T0360317

AUSTRALIAN HOMESCHOOLING SERIES

Test Your Spelling 7 & 8

Years 7 – 10

CORONEOS PUBLICATIONS

Item No 568

No part of this publication may be reproduced, stored in a retrieval system or transmitted in any form or by any means, electronic, mechanical, photocopying, recording or otherwise, without the prior permission of the copyright owner.

This book is available from recognised booksellers or contact:

Coroneos Publications

Telephone: (02) 9838 9265   **Facsimile:** (02) 9838 8982
Business Address: 2/195 Prospect Highway Seven Hills 2147
Website: www.coroneos.com.au
E-mail: info@fivesenseseducation.com.au

Item # 568
Test Your Spelling 7 & 8
by Valerie Marett
First published 2019

ISBN: 978-1-922034-77-9
© Valerie Marett

Test Your Spelling 7 & 8

<u>How to Use This Book</u>
Score each page. Write the scores in the box. Mark as you go.

Each section indicates skills passed or failed. Answers are at the back of the book. <u>Complete one section at a time.</u> Your child may use a dictionary.

Do not help your child other than reading the words for the spelling test at the beginning of each unit. <u>Do not proceed to the next section if your child has failed to gain the required score.</u>

Instructions on how to use the scores to discover which books are necessary to improve your child's knowledge are given below.

Section 1

1	2	3	4	5	6	7	8	9	10
11	12	13	14	15	16	17	18	19	20
21	22	23	24	25	26				

Score: /844
Pass: 649/837

Section 2

1	2	3	4	5	6	7	8	9	10
11	12	13	14	15	16	17	18	19	20
21	22	23	24	25	26	27	28		

Score: /908
Pass: 707/919

To assess results go to page 2.

Section 1

644 or above: proceed to Section 2 of the test.

422 — 649
work through *Successful Spelling 6*.

361—422
work through **Successful Spelling 5** and *Revise Your Phonics 1 & 2.*

Below 361
Your child needs help with spelling and phonics. It is suggested that you work through **Revise Your Phonics 1 & 2** that may indicate gaps that may require your child to work through some of the **Learn to Read, Write and Spell** books and then look at **Successful Spelling 4 or 5.**

Section 2

707 or above
The child has mastered their spelling.

454 — 706
Work through **Successful Spelling 7** and *Revise Your Phonics 1 & 2*

Below 360
While your child may have passed Section 1 of this test **Successful Spelling 7** is likely to be too hard for them. It is recommended that you first work through **Revise Your Phonics 1** and **Revise Your Phonics 2** and then proceed to **Successful Spelling 6**.

Section 1, Test 1: Common spelling rules

Complete the rules below: (1 point each)

1. a is sounded as the short o after _____, _____ and _____.

2. If y comes at the beginning of a word or syllable it is a _____; if
it is the only vowel at the end of a one syllable word it has the _____
sound; if y is the only vowel at the end of a word of more than one syllable
it has the _____ sound.

3. Every syllable must have a _____.

4. When we double m or n we often write _____ to complete the syllable.

5. When a word ends with an f sound to make it plural we _____ and
add a _____.

6. When g is followed by e, i or y it often makes the ____ sound.

7. When c is followed by e, i or y it often makes the ____ sound.

8. c is usually followed by _____, _____, and _____; k is usually followed by
___, and ___; ck comes after a _____.

9. dge and tch are used only after a _____.

10. i before e except after _____ , but only when it says _____.

11. We usually double f. l, s and z after a _____.

12. When adding an ending to a silent e, _____ and add an
ending _____.

13. Keep the e of a word that ends in ge or ce when adding the suffixes
_____ or _____.

14. When a noun ends with s, ss, sh, ch, x or z add _____ to form the plural.

15. When making a plural from nouns ending in o, if the word ends in a
consonant we add ____; if the word has a foreign origin we add ___.

16. When a word ends in ie, change the word to ____ before adding a suffix.

Score: /30   **Pass: 23/30**

Section 1, Test 2: short a sound

A. Spell these words. (Adult to read. 1 point each.)

abeyance	acquisition	acquittal	adjudicate
admirable	allegation	alliance	anxiety
analysis	anticipation	appal	appreciate
appropriate	assassinate	assent	atrocious
callous	caricature	castigate	fascinate

B. Complete these rules for syllables. (1 point each space)

1. Every syllable must have a _____.

2. When the word has a prefix, divide the word between the _____ and the _____, e.g., un/fair

3. When a word has a suffix, divide the word between the _____ and the _____ if the suffix has a _____, e.g., fear/less.

4. When two or more consonants come _____ two vowels, the word is usually divided between the _____ consonants, e.g., bet/ter

C. Divide the following words into syllables. (1 point each)

1. assassinate _____   2. appal _____

3. anticipation _____   4. acquittal_____

5. allegation _____   6. callous _____

D. Complete the following table. (1 point each space)

	noun	adjective	verb
1.	_____	_____	fascinate
2.	allegation	_____	_____
3.	_____	_____	appreciate
4.	_____	admirable	_____

Score: /32   **Pass: 22/32**

© Valerie Marett
Coroneos Publications

Australian Homeschooling #568
Test Your Spelling 7 & 8

Section 1, Test 3: short a sound

A. Find a word from the list on page 4 to match each definition below. (1 point)

1. hardened, insensitive _____

2. fill with alarm or horror, dismay, displease _____

3. shockingly wicked or cruel; very bad or lacking in taste _____

4. separation of something into its basic parts in order to discover its nature or meaning _____

5. the act of foreseeing or realising beforehand _____

6. to agree to _____

7. a picture, description etc ludicrously exaggerating the peculiarities or defects of people or things _____

8. the act of gaining possession of something _____

9. to act as a judge in a competition; to pronounce or pass judgement _____

10. a finding or verdict of not guilty in a criminal trial _____

B. Rules: complete each rule below. (1 point each space)

1. The prefixes –ab, –ac, -ad, -ag, -al, -ap, -as, and -at all mean _____,

   _____, _____, _____, _____.

2. If y is the only vowel at the end of a word of more that one syllable it has

   the _____ sound,

3. The suffix "—ate" can have several meanings: as a noun it means

   _____, _____or _____, e.g., candidate; as a

   verb it means _____, e.g., graduate; as an adjective it

   means _____, e.g., inviolate.

4. The suffix —less means _____.

Score: /22   **Pass: 17/22**

Section 1, Test 4: short b and c (k) sound

A. Spell these words. (Adult to read. 1 point each.)

believable	beneficial	benevolent	bequeath
bewildered	bilateral	bludgeon	boisterous
boycott	brevity	buoyancy	bureaucracy
commotion	conceived	connection	consciousness
consequences	convince	critical	curiosity

B. Write the base word of each spelling word below. (1 point each)

1. critical _____

2. beneficial _____

3. connection _____

4. consciousness _____

5. buoyancy _____

6. bewildered _____

C. Find a word from the spelling list to match each definition below. (1 point)

1. to form an idea, to imagine _____

2. the power to float or rise in a liquid _____

3. the act or fact following as a result of something
    before it _____

4. relating to or affecting two sides or parties _____

5. to join together in preventing dealings with
    so as to frighten or force _____

6. inner understanding of something, knowledge
    of one's own feelings, existence etc. _____

7. a system of administration marked by centralisation
    of authority _____

8. shortness of time _____

9. wishing to do good for others _____

10. to give personal property to a beneficiary
    under a will _____

11. a violent or wild and noisy motion _____

Score: /37   Pass: 27/37

© Valerie Marett
Coroneos Publications

Australian Homeschooling #568
Test Your Spelling 7 & 8

Section 1, Test 5: short b and c (k) sound

A. Complete these rules. (1 point each space)

1. The prefix con— and com— mean _____, _____, _____
    e.g., converge, completely.

2. The prefix un— means _____ or _____, e.g., uncontrolled.

3. The prefix bio— means _____, e.g., biology.

B. Write the adjectival form of the following nouns. (1 point each)

1. bureaucracy _____   2. consciousness _____

3. buoyancy _____   4. beneficiary _____

5. consequence _____

C. Write the adverbial form of the following words. (1 point each)

1. consequence _____   2. convince _____

3. believable _____   4. conceived _____

D. Two of the adverbs you have just formed can be changed into antonyms by adding the prefix un—. Write them below.

1. _____   2. _____

E. Find a spelling word from page 6 that is a synonym of each set of words below:

1. acceptable, credible, plausible, imaginable   _____

2. censorious, derogatory, disapproving, scathing   _____

3. assure, persuade, satisfy, sway   _____

4. briefness, conciseness, curtness, succinctness   _____

5. inquisitiveness, interest, nosiness   _____

6. bash, batter, buffet, clout, thrash, whack   _____

F. Write the antonym of each word below. (1 point each)

1. critical _____   2. curiosity _____

Score: /25   **Pass: 18/25**

7

© Valerie Marett
Coroneos Publications

Australian Homeschooling #568
Test Your Spelling 7 & 8

Section 1, Test 6: c that says s, de-, dis-, in-, re-

A. Spell these words. (Adult to read. 1 point each.)

censure	conceit	concentration	conceptualise
conciliate	deceptive	deduction	defray
deleterious	deficit	definitive	derivation
deviate	dilapidated	diminish	disguised
dispel	intercept	resistance	vaccinate

B. Complete the following: (1 point each space)

1. If y is the only vowel at the end of a word of more than one _____

   it has the _____ sound, e.g., berry.

2. The prefix con— and com— mean _____, e.g., converge, completely.

3. Con— is used before a consonant but is never used before _____.

C. Choose an antonym from your spelling words for each word below.

1. compliance _____	2. incite _____
3. surplus _____	4. adhere to _____
5. heighten _____	6. modesty _____
7. beneficial _____	8. approbation _____
9. trustworthy _____	

D. Change each word below so that it ends with the suffix —tion. (1 point each)

1. deviate _____	2. conciliate _____
3. conceptualise _____	4. deceptive _____
5. intercept _____	6. vaccinate _____
7. dilapidated _____	

E. Divide each word below into syllables.

1. deleterious _____	2. disguised _____

Score: /42   Pass: 34/42

© Valerie Marett
Coroneos Publications

Australian Homeschooling #568
Test Your Spelling 7 & 8

Section 1, Test 7: c that says s, de-, dis-, in-, re-

A. Solve the crossword by finding a synonym from your spelling list on page 8.
(1 point each answer.)

Across
1. adjudicate, mediate
3. decline, decrease
7. hindrance, obstruction
9. visualise, imagine
10. arrogance, boastfulness
11. criticism, rebuke

Down
2. single-mindedness, absorption
3. conclusive, decisive
4. block, stop, cut off
5. beginning, inception
6. misleading, delusive
8. cover, meet, pay for

B. Add "ed" and "ing" to each word below to change the word to past tense or a participle. You may need to change the word slightly. (2 points each question)

		ed	ing
1.	censure	_____	_____
2.	resistance	_____	_____
3.	defray	_____	_____
4.	concentration	_____	_____

Score: /20   Pass: 16/20

Section 1, Test 8: d, el-, em-, ex-

A. Spell these words. (Adult to read. 1 point each.)

digestible	disagreeable	disastrous	distinguished
distributed	durable	duress	dynamics
eccentricity	elementary	eloquent	embarrass
embezzle	emigrate	estuary	exaggeration
excruciating	exhausted	extraordinary	extravagance

B. Complete the following: (1 point each space)

1. The prefix ex–, e– or ef- mean "_____, _____, _____ or _____" and are used before the vowels _____.

2. The suffixes —ant and —ent mean "_____, _____, or _____," e.g., assistant—one who assists.

3. The prefixes em— and en— mean "_____, _____, _____, _____, or _____."

4. The suffixes —ar and —ary mean "_____ or _____."

C. Find an antonym from the words in the spelling list for each word below. (1 point each)

1. fragile	_____	2. immigrate	_____
3. invigorated	_____	4. affable	_____
5. economical	_____	6. ordinariness	_____
7. mild	_____	8. understatement	_____
9. auspicious	_____	10. advanced	_____

D. Change each word below to an adjective. (1 point each)

1. embarrass	_____	2. exaggeration	_____
3. eccentricity	_____	4. extravagance	_____

E. Write a sentence using the word "dynamics" correctly. (2 points)

_____

Score: /51   Pass: 44/51

Section 1, Test 9: d, el-, em-, ex-

A. Find a word from the spelling list on page 10 that is a synonym of each list of words below. (1 point each)

1. coercion, compulsion, force, pressure   _____

2. astonishing, notable, outstanding, uncommon   _____

3. eminent, renowned, prominent, famous   _____

4. agonising, intense, acute, severe, intolerable   _____

5. articulate, expressive, fluent, forceful, persuasive _____

6. abnormal, oddity, idiosyncratic, unconventional   _____

7. allocated, apportioned, dispensed, circulated   _____

8. misappropriate, steal, purloin, skim   _____

9. hard wearing, indestructible, strong, sturdy   _____

10. calamitous, catastrophic, devastating, dreadful _____

B. Words can also be used in legal, business or geographical terms. Use a dictionary to find the meanings of each word below. Write the meaning next to the word. (2 points each)

1. embezzle (business): _____

_____

2. duress (legal): _____

_____

3. estuary (geographical): _____

_____

C. Divide each word below into syllables. (1 point each)

1.	excruciating _____	2. duress	_____
3.	disagreeable _____	4. eloquent	_____
5.	dynamics _____	6. extravagance	_____

Score: /22   Pass: 16/22

Section 1, Test 10: short e, em-, en-, er-, es-, ex-, f, for-, fore, g

A. Spell these words. (Adult to read. 1 point each.)

effervescent	encyclopaedia	embezzlement	exorbitant
expiate	exquisite	extravagance	exuberant
farcical	fascinating	fatigue	ferocious
fiord	forecast	forfeit	fraudulent
gaiety	garble	geology	germane

B. Complete the following: (1 point each space)

1. The prefix ex–, e– or ef– mean "_____, _____, _____ or

    _____" and are used before the vowels and _____.

2. The prefix fore— means "_____, _____, e.g., foreclose.

3. The prefix for— means "_____, _____, e.g., forbid.

C. Some of the words in your spelling list on this page have legal, geographical or english meanings in addition to their normal meaning. Write the meaning of each word in the space provided. (2 points each)

1. **geology** (geography): _____

    _____

2. **encyclopaedia** (English): _____

    _____

3. **fiord** (geography) : _____

    _____

4. **fraud** (legal): _____

    _____

D. Two of your spelling words can only be used as adjectives and can not be changed to nouns, verbs or adverbs. Write them below. Use one of the words in a sentence. (1 point each)

1. _____   2. _____

_____

Score: /41   Pass: 32/41

© Valerie Marett
Coroneos Publications

Australian Homeschooling #568
Test Your Spelling 7 & 8

Section 1, Test 11: short e, em-, en-, er-, es-, ex-, f, for-, fore, g

A. **Find a synonym from your spelling list on page 12 to match each line of synonyms below.** (1 point each)

1.   bizarreness, idiosyncrasy, quirk, unconventionality _____

2.   absurd, comical, laughable, ludicrous, nonsensical _____

3.   lose, relinquish, give up, renounce, surrender _____

4.   distort, jumble, mix-up, corrupt _____

5.   cheerfulness, fun, happiness, merriment, revelry _____

6.   boisterous, lively, vivacious, high-spirited _____

7.   pertinent, relevant, related, connected _____

8.   flawless, impeccable, perfect, rare, superb _____

B. Write an antonym to match each spelling word below. (1 point each)

1.   eccentricity _____   2. germane _____

3.   exuberant _____   4. ferocious _____

5.   fraudulent _____   6. fatigue _____

C. Find a spelling word from the list on page 12 to match each definition below.
(1 point each)

1.   of great interest or attraction, enchanting _____

2.   going beyond what is normal, right or reasonable _____

3.   to give an opinion about, predict _____

4.   savagely fierce _____

D. Write the plural of the following words. (1 point each)

1. eccentricity _____   2. estuary _____

3. encyclopaedia _____

Score: /21   Pass: 16/21

Section 1, Test 12: g, gu, h, hy—,im—, in—

A. Spell these words. (Adult to read. 1 point each.)

glossary	gorgeous	gauge	guarantee
haemorrhage	harangue	harass	heinous
hideous	hierarchy	horde	hypocrisy
imaginary	immediately	independence	indulge
instantaneous	intelligence	interfere	interrupt

B. Complete the following: (1 point each space)

1. The prefix im— is a variant of il— and in— meaning "_____, _____" when used before _____, e.g., immoral.

2. The prefix in—, il—, im—, ir— can also mean " ___, _____, _____, _____," e.g., influence.

3. When the word has a prefix, divide the word between _____ and _____, e.g., un/fair. When the word has a suffix, divide the word between _____ and _____ if the suffix has a _____ sound, e.g.., fear/less.

4. The prefix hyper— means _____, _____, _____, _____, _____, e.g., hyperactive.

5. The prefix hypo— means "_____ or _____" e.g., hypodermic.

6. The prefix haemo— and hemo— means "_____", e.g., haematology.

C. Words are often misused. Explain the difference between the two words below.
(2 points each)

1. harangue:_____

2. harass: _____

D. Divide each word below into syllables. (1 point each)

1. hideous _____ 2. immediately _____

3. guarantee _____ 4. haemorrhage _____

Score: /48   Pass: 35/48

© Valerie Marett
Coroneos Publications

Australian Homeschooling #568
Test Your Spelling 7 & 8

Section 1, Test 13: g, gu, h, hy—,im—, in—

A. Find a spelling word from the list on page 14 to match each definition below.
(1 point each)

1.	hateful, reprehensible, odious, atrocious	_____
2.	to yield to the wishes of oneself	_____
3.	the act of pretending to have a character, belief or principles one does not have	_____
4.	any system or people organised in grades or ranks	_____
5.	to bleed severely	_____
6.	to judge, to estimate	_____
7.	at once, without delay	_____
8.	done or completed in an instant	_____
9.	a list of basic technical and difficult words in a subject or field with definitions	_____

B. Write the antonym of each spelling word below. (1 point each)

1.	intelligence _____	2. gorgeous	_____
3.	hideous _____	4. hypocrisy	_____
5.	imaginary _____	6. indulge	_____

C. Write the homonym of the spelling word below. Explain the different meanings of each word. (3 points total)

1.	horde _____

_____

_____

D. Change the following words into adverbs. (1 point each)

1.	instantaneous _____	2. intelligence _____

Score: /20   **Pass: 15/20**

Section 1, Test 14: j, l, m, mega—, mis—, mono—

A. Spell these words. (Adult to read. 1 point each.)

jealousy	judgement	jurisdiction	juvenile
legislation	liable	liquefy	luscious
magnificent	manoeuvre	megabyte	meridian
meticulous	miscellaneous	misdemeanour	monoloque
naturally	nautical	necessity	negotiation

B. Complete the following: (1 point each space)

1. J is only ever used at the _____ of a word and never at the

   _____.

2. The prefix mis— means "_____, _____ or _____", e.g.,
   misunderstanding, misspelling. It can also mean "_____, _____"
   e.g., mistrust.

3. The prefix mega— means "_____, _____ or _____"
   e.g., megalith, megaton.

C. Some of the words in the spelling list have other meanings of a geographical, legal, computing or English nature. Write the meaning of each word below. (2 points each)

1. **monologue** (english) : _____

   _____

2. **legislation** (legal): _____

   _____

3. **meridian** (geography): _____

   _____

4. **jurisdiction** (legal): _____

5. **megabyte** (computer): _____

   _____

6. **misdemeanour** (legal): _____

7. **judgement** (legal): _____

Score: /44   Pass: 35/44

© Valerie Marett
Coroneos Publications

Australian Homeschooling #568
Test Your Spelling 7 & 8

Section 1, Test 15: j, l, m, mega—, mis—, mono—

A. Find a synonym from page 16 to match each line of words below. (1 point each space)

1. child-like, immature, youthful _____

2. essential, need, requirement, requisite _____

3. condense, melt, thaw, deliquesce _____

4. marine, maritime, sea-going _____

5. delicious, rich, succulent, delectable _____

6. move, edge, guide, navigate, steer _____

7. accountable, responsible, answerable _____

8. excellent, extraordinary, exquisite, glorious _____

9. accurate, careful, exact, methodical _____

10. assorted, mixed, sundry, various _____

B. Change the following words to an adjective. (1 point each)

1. jurisdiction _____   2. manoeuvre _____

3. necessity _____   4. meridian _____

5. jealousy _____   6. naturally _____

C. Change the following words to an adverbs. (1 point each)

1. meticulous _____   2. necessity _____

3. magnificent _____

D. Write the meaning of each homonym below. (2 point each)

1. liable: _____

2. libel: _____

E. Write a sentence using one of the homonyms in exercise D correctly. (2 points)

Score: /25   Pass: 18/25

Section 1, Test 16: n, non—, long o, short o

A. Spell these words. (Adult to read. 1 point each.)

coercion	cognisant	complacent	idiosyncrasy
incongruous	innocuous	monotonous	nocturnal
nominee	nonsense	notoriety	nuisance
obliterate	onerous	oppression	potential
proficient	pronounceable	solicitude	spontaneity

B. Complete the following: (1 point each space)

1. The prefixes cog—, col—, com— and cor— mean "_____ or

    _____," e.g., cognate, collaborate, commitment, correct.

2. The prefix pro— means "_____ or _____," e.g., protocol.

3. a, e, o and u are usually long _____.

4. The prefix non— means "_____", e.g., nondescript.

C. Complete the passage below using appropriate words from your spelling list.
(Hint: you may need to change the form of the word.)   (1 point each space)

1. The students found the _____ tone of the teacher hard to listen

    to in the _____ heat.

2. The _____ of the storeman was obvious to all.

3. The _____ visit of the possum had become such a

    _____ that John required no further _____ from his
    wife before he contacted the Council regarding its removal.

4. The old man's _____ behaviour, while _____,
    was very trying at times.

5. I am fully _____ with all the rules and regulations governing
    the keeping of pets.

6. The _____ of the Minister was now so great that it had the

    _____ to seriously embarrass the Government.

7. The _____ _____ of my friend comforted me and

    made the task of organising the funeral less _____.

Score: /40   **Pass: 32/40**

© Valerie Marett
Coroneos Publications

Australian Homeschooling #568
Test Your Spelling 7 & 8

Section 1, Test 17: n, non—, long o, short o

A.   Write an antonym for each spelling word below. (1 point each)

1. proficient   _____   2. incongruous   _____

3. nonsense   _____   4. pronounceable _____

5. complacent   _____   6. nocturnal   _____

7. monotonous   _____

B. Choose a synonym from the spelling list on page 18 to fit each line of synonyms below. (1 point)

1.   concern, consideration, thoughtfulness   _____

2.   cancel, eradicate, erase,   _____

3.   impetuousness, impulsiveness, automatic   _____

4.   ability, aptitude, capability, promise   _____

5.   inappropriate, incompatible, inconsistent   _____

6.   duress, intimidation, restraint, force   _____

7.   annoyance, irritant, bother, trouble   _____

8.   burdensome, difficult, exacting, arduous   _____

C. Write the adverbial form of each word below. (1 point only)

1.   spontaneity _____   2. nocturnal _____

3.   solicitude _____   4. oppression _____

5.   notoriety   _____   6. complacent _____

7.   proficient _____   8. monotonous _____

D. Divide these words into syllables. (1 point each)

1.   cognisant _____   2. obliterate _____

3.   onerous   _____   4. solicitude _____

Score: /27   Pass: 20/27

Section 1, Test 18: long a, a that says ar, ar, qu, r, re-

A. Spell these words. (Adult to read. 1 point each.)

ache	application	Arctic	articulate
gnarled	particular	passable	quadruplicate
quarantine	quarrel	queue	quiescent
quorum	realise	recommendation	recurrence
regularly	reluctantly	responsible	sarcasm
scrupulous	separable	simultaneous	specialise

B. Complete the following: (1 point each space)

1. q is never found in the English language _____.

2. The prefixes quad— and quat— mean "_____," e.g., quadrangle, quadruplets.

3. The prefix re— means to "_____," e.g., redo; it also means "_____", e.g., revert.

4. The suffixes —ous, —eous, —ose, —ious mean "_____, _____, e.g., adventurous, courageous.

5. The prefixes spec—, spect—, spi— and spic— all mean "_____," e.g., specimen, spectator, conspicuous.

6. The prefixes sub—, suc—, suf—, sup—, sur— and sus— all mean " _____, _____, _____, _____, _____,

C. Choose a synonym from you word list to match each word below. (1 point each)

1. distinct _____
2. understand _____
3. acceptable _____
4. gnarled _____
5. conscientious _____
6. repeatedly _____
7. periodic _____
8. passive _____
9. concurrent _____
10. culpable _____

D. Two spelling words have similar meanings. Write them below. (1 point each)

1. _____
2. _____

Score: /47   **Pass: 38/48**

© Valerie Marett
Coroneos Publications

Australian Homeschooling #568
Test Your Spelling 7 & 8

Section 1, Test 19: long a, a that says ar, ar, qu, r, re-

A. Choose an antonym from your spelling list on page 20 to match each antonym below. (1 point each)

1.	unsatisfactory	_____	2. unscrupulous	_____
3.	sporadically	_____	4. inseparable	_____
5.	isolated	_____	6. active	_____

B. Choose a spelling word on page 20 to match each definition below. (1 point)

1. the quality of being usable for a special purpose   _____

2. one of four copies or identical items, especially
   typed material   _____

3. harsh or bitter words intended to hurt another person,
   especially by saying the opposite of what is meant   _____

4. a line of people or vehicles awaiting their turn   _____

5. a suggestion as to the best cause of action   _____

6. the minimum number of people that must be in
   attendance before a formal meeting can proceed   _____

7. to speak words clearly   _____

8. being at rest, quiet or still   _____

9. having or showing a strict regard for what is right   _____

10. existing, happening or operating at the same time   _____

C. Write the two adverbs contained in your spelling list on page 20. (1 point each)

1.	_____	2. _____

D. Write the base word of each word below. (1 point)

1. recommendation	_____	2. application	_____
2. specialise	_____	4. scrupulous	_____
5. passable	_____	6. recurrence	_____

Score: /24   Pass: 19/24

Section 1, Test 20: sub-, sup-, syn-, tem-, tran, trib-, un-

A. Spell these words. (Adult to read. 1 point each.)

subsequent	suddenness	superstitious	synonymous
temperament	temporarily	topography	tranquillity
treachery	tributaries	trough	tyranny
ulterior	umbrage	unanimous	unconscious
unconscionable	uncorroborated	unparalleled	unpronounceable

B. Complete the following: (1 point each space)

1. The prefix un— means "_____, _____, _____," e.g.,
   unceasing, unequal.

2. The prefix under— means "_____, _____" or "_____
   _____," e.g., underprivileged. It also means
   "_____," e.g., underpass.

3. The prefixes tem— or tempo— mean "_____" e.g., contemporary.

4. The prefixes ten— and tin— mean "_____" e.g., tenant.

5. The prefix trans— means "_____, _____,
   _____," e.g., transform, transmit.

6. The prefix tor—, tors— or tort— means "_____ "e.g.,
   torture.

7. The prefixes sub—, suc—, suf—, sup—, sur— and sus— all mean
   "_____, _____, _____, _____,
   _____," e.g., sustain, survive, support, succeed, submarine.

**C. Three of the spelling words have geographical meanings. Write each word and
its meaning below.** (2 points each question.)

1. _____ _____
   _____

2. _____ _____

3. _____ _____
   _____

Score: /45   Pass: 36/45

Section 1, Test 21: sub-, sup-, syn-, tem-, tran, trib-, un-

A. Choose a word from the spelling list on page 22 that fits each definition below.
(1 point each)

1. unconfirmed, uncertain _____

2. someone who believes in something not
    based on reason or knowledge _____

3. of one mind, in complete agreement _____

4. occurring or coming later or after _____

5. not permanent _____

6. offence given or taken _____

7. the act of breaking faith or trust _____

8. complete unchecked abuse of power;
    despotic abuse of authority _____

9. having the same meaning or quality as _____

10. peacefulness, calm _____

B. Write a sentence that shows your understanding of the meaning and use of each word below. (2 point each.)

1. unconscious: _____

    _____

2. unconscionable: _____

    _____

C. Write an antonym for each word below. (1 point each.)

1. unpronounceable _____ 2. temporarily _____

3. suddenness _____ 4. unconscious _____

D. Write the adjectival form of each word below. (1 point each)

1. suddenness _____ 2. temperament _____

Score: /20   Pass: 15/20

Section 1, Test 22: v sound, Foreign Plurals, Confused Words

A. Spell these words. (Adult to read. 1 point each.)

vacuum	vague	variegated	vengeance
versatility	vicinity	vicious	voracious
antithesis	curriculum	criterion	formula
hypothesis	radius	stratum	terminus
bias	prejudice	compel	impel
effective	efficient	equable	equitable
illegal	unlawful	per capita	per head
perpetually	continually	principle	principal

B. Complete the following: (2 points each)

The suffixes —ous, —eous, —ose and —ious mean _____

_____, e.g., adventurous, courageous, verbose,
fractious.

C. Write the plural form of these words: (1 point each)

1. hypothesis _____   2. curriculum _____

3. criterion _____   4. radius _____

5. stratum _____   6. formula _____

7. antithesis _____   8. terminus _____

D. Write a sentence showing you understand the meaning of each pair of word below. (2 points each question)

1. per capita:_____

   per head: _____

2. principle: _____

   principal: _____

3. bias: _____

   prejudice: _____

Score: /50   **Pass: 38/50**

© Valerie Marett
Coroneos Publications

Australian Homeschooling #568
Test Your Spelling 7 & 8

Section 1, Test 23: v sound, Foreign Plurals, Confused Words

A. Choose a word from the spelling list on page 24 to fit each definition below: (1 point each.)

1. the ability to turn with ease from one task to another

2. a line segment from the centre of a circle or sphere to its perimeter

3. fair, reasonable, just

4. region near or about a place

5. a standard rule or principle for testing anything

6. continually, lasting for ever

7. idea, theory or statement adopted as a starting point for discussion, experimentation etc.

8. to drive or urge forward

9. eager or greedy in some area

10. a person or thing that is directly opposite to someone or something else

B. Choose a synonym from the spelling list on page 24 to fit each group of words below. (1 point each)

1. programme, syllabus, course

2. coerce, constrain, drive, force

3. marbled, multi-coloured, mottled

4. ambiguous, imprecise, unclear

5. depot, station

6. reprisal, requital, retaliation

7. capable, competent, productive

Score: /17   **Pass: 13/17**

© Valerie Marett
Coroneos Publications

Australian Homeschooling #568
Test Your Spelling 7 & 8

Section 1, Test 24: more Frequently Confused Words
Noun to Adjective: —ible or —able

A. Spell these words. (Adult to read. 1 point each.)

astrology	astronomy	compliment	complement
depreciate	deprecate	detract	distract
ingenuous	ingenious	luxuriant	luxurious
perspective	prospective	precipitate	precipitous
admission	admissible	combustion	combustible
corruption	corruptible	deduction	deductible
exhaustion	exhaustible	expansion	expansible
permission	permissible	suppression	suppressible
commendation	commendable	explication	explicable
inflammation	inflammable	irritation	irritable
justification	justifiable	penetration	penetrable
separation	separable	toleration	tolerable

B. Complete the following: (1 point each space)

1. If a noun ends in "-ion" rather than "-ation" the adjective usually ends in
   _____, or in an adverb, _____," e.g., demonstration becomes
   demonstrable or demonstrably.

2. If a noun ends in "-ation" the adjective usually ends in _____ or in
   an adverb, _____e.g., demonstration becomes demonstrable.

3. The suffix —able is often, but not always, added to _____ such
   as agree, (agreeable); to _____,
   e.g., cure becomes curable; to _____,
   e.g., rely becomes reliable.

C. Change the word to the form requested: (1 point each)

1. justification (adj)_____   2. suppression (adj)_____

3. ingenious (n)_____   4. distract (n) _____

5. corruption (adj)_____   6. expansion (v)_____

7. inflammable (v) _____   8. distract (n) _____

Score: /63   Pass: 52/63

© Valerie Marett
Coroneos Publications

Australian Homeschooling #568
Test Your Spelling 7 & 8

Section 1, Test 25: more Frequently Confused Words
Noun to Adjective: —ible or —able

A. Add "—ible" or "—able" to these root stems. (1 point each)

1.	elig _____	2. cap	_____
3.	irrit _____	4. memor	_____
5.	ami _____	6. leg	_____

B. Choose a word from the spelling list on page 26 to fit each definition below. (1 point each)

1. to state earnest disapproval of, urge reasons against   _____

2. easily aroused or excited to passion or anger   _____

3. likely to happen at a future date   _____

4. open, straight forward; sometimes easily deceived   _____

5. able to catch fire and burn easily   _____

6. plentiful or strong in growth   _____

7. an award involving special praise   _____

8. to take away part as from quality or reward   _____

9. the practise of deliberately allowing or permitting
    a thing of which one disapproves   _____

10. to drain of strength or property, deplete   _____

C. Write an antonym for each word below: (1 point each)

1.	admission _____	2. irritable	_____
3.	separation _____	4. tolerable	_____
5.	corruption _____	6. permission	_____

D. Write a synonym for the synonyms below: (1 point)

accelerate, bring on, hasten   _____

Score: /23   **Pass: 18/23**

Section 2

Before proceeding to Section 2 score and add up tests 1-26. If you child has not scored 649 or above do not proceed to Section 2.

Section 2, Test 1, Common Spelling rules

Complete the rules below. (Points as indicated.)

1. Every syllable must have a _____. (1 point)

2. The prefix dynam– means _____. (1 point)

3. The prefix cata– means _____. (1 point)

4. When nouns end in y and are proceeded by a vowel, to form a plural _____. When nouns end in y and are proceeded by a consonant _____. When proper nouns end in y the plural is formed by adding _____. (2 points)

5. The prefixes com– and con– mean _____, _____ or _____. (1½ points)

6. The prefixes in– or im– mean _____, _____, _____ or _____ (2 points)

7. The prefixes dis-- and dif– mean _____, _____, _____ _____, _____, _____. (3 points)

8. The prefix hyper- means _____, _____. (1 point)

9. The prefix hypo– means _____, _____, _____. (1½ pt)

10. The prefix pre– means _____ and the prefix pro- means _____, _____. (1½ points)

11. The prefix un– means _____, _____, _____. (1½ pt)

12. The prefix re– means _____ or _____. (1 points)

13. The prefix magn— means _____ and the prefix mono– means _____. (1 points)

14. The prefix trans– means _____, _____, or _____ (1½ pt)

15. The prefixes dem– and demo– mean _____, _____ _____. (1½ points)

Score: /22   **Pass: 18/22**

© Valerie Marett
Coroneos Publications

Australian Homeschooling #508
Test Your Spelling 7 & 8

Section 2, Test 2: -ity, -ory, -ogy, -ary

A. Spell these words. (Adult to read. 1 point each.)

alacrity	austerity	congruity	disparity
duplicity	equanimity	gullibility	perversity
probity	proclivity		
conciliatory	derogatory	desultory	ideology
morphology	ophthalmology	tautology	
complementary	complimentary	quandary	rudimentary

B. Divide each word below into syllables. (1 point each)

1. complementary _____
2. desultory _____
3. duplicity _____
4. tautology _____
5. ophthalmology _____
6. quandry _____

C. Noun, verb, adjective or adverb? Complete. (1 point)

All the spelling words listed above that end with –ity are _____

D. Explain the difference in meaning between the two words. (1 point each.)

1. complementary: _____
2. complimentary: _____

D. Complete the chart. (1 point each space)

Noun	Adjective	Adverb
1. austerity	_____	_____
2. _____	conciliatory	_____
3. _____	desultory	_____
4. congruity	_____	
5. disparity	_____	_____
6. morphology	_____	_____
7. gullibility	_____	_____

Score: /46   **Pass:** 38/46

© Valerie Marett
Coroneos Publications

Australian Homeschooling #568
Test Your Spelling 7 & 8

Section 2, Test 3: -ity, -ory, -ogy, -ary

A. Choose a word from the spelling list on page 30 to fit each definition below.
  (1 point each)

1. a phrase or expression in which the same thing is said twice in different words _____

2. relating to an immature, undeveloped or basic form _____

3. a great difference between two or more things _____

4. a tendency to choose or do something regularly _____

5. deceitfulness _____

6. the study of a particular form, shape or structure _____

7. a difficult situation, a practical dilemma _____

8. occurring randomly or occasionally _____

9. the quality of having strong moral principles; honesty and decency _____

10. brisk and cheerful readiness _____

11. the quality of two things being agreement or harmony _____

12. a lack of social awareness where one is easily deceived or cheated _____

B. Write the plural of each word below. (1 point each)

1. ideology _____   2. complementary _____

3. quandary _____   4. congruity _____

5. perversity _____   6. tautology _____

B. Write the antonym of each word below. (1 point each)

1. complimentary _____   2. austerity _____

3. derogatory _____   4. gullibility _____

Score: /22   Pass: 18/22

© Valorie Marett
Coroneos Publications

Australian Homeschooling #568
Test Your Spelling 7 & 8

Section 2, Test 4: y says -ee, y says short i, y says long i

A. Spell these words. (Adult to read. 1 point each.)

calumny	consistency	corollary	dichotomy
hegemony	ignominy	oxymoron	pithy
soliloquy	trichotomy		
acronym	androgynous	cryptic	cynicism
dysfunctional	eponym	idiosyncratic	idyllic
mythology	synecdoche		
cyclical	dynamic	paroxysm	vilify

B. Complete: (1 point each space.)

1. _____ is often used when there is no other vowel. Then it makes the

   _____ sound.

2. If y is the only vowel at the end of a word of _____ syllable

   then it has the _____ sound, e.g., berry.

3. When a word ends in y and you add a _____ beginning with i you

   keep the _____, e.g., supplying

4. To make a plural if a word ends in y and there is a _____ before

   the y change _____ and add _____, e.g., cherries.

C. Write the plural of each word below. (1 point each.)

1, ignominy	_____	2. synecdoche	_____
3. eponym	_____	4. idiosyncratic	_____
5. acronym	_____	6. corollary	_____

D. Write the antonym for each word. (1 point each.)

1. corollary	_____	2. ignominy	_____
3. cynicism	_____	4. hegemony	_____
5. idyllic	_____	6. dynamic	_____

Score: /45   Pass: 18/45

Section 2, Test 5: y says -ee, y says short i, y says long I

A. Choose a word from the spelling list on page 32 to fit each definition below.
(1 point each)

1. a figure of speech where apparently contradictory terms appear in conjunction _____

2. a division or contrast between two things that are or are represented as being opposed or entirely different _____

3. having a meaning that is mysterious or obscure _____

4. a sudden attack or outburst of a particular emotion or activity _____

5. a figure of speech in which a part is made to represent the whole or visa versa _____

6. having both male and female characteristics _____

7. a person after whom a discovery is named _____

8. an inclination to believe that people are motivated purely by self-interest, scepticism _____

9. leadership or dominance, especially by one state or social group over another _____

10. a word or name formed as an abbreviation from the initial component in a phrase or word, usually individual letters, e.g., CSIRO _____

11. a division into three categories _____

12. the making of false or defamatory statements about someone in order to damage their reputation _____

B. Write a synonym for each word below. (1 point each)

1. mythology _____		2. dynamic _____
3. dichotomy _____		4. idiosyncratic _____
5. idyllic _____		6. cyclical _____

Score: /18   Pass: 14/18

Section 2, Test 6: -tion

A. Spell these words. (Adult to read. 1 point each.)

abrogation	asphyxiation	circumlocution	conflagration
depreciation	depredation	diminution	equivocation
gesticulation	homogenisation	inauguration	inundation
marginalisation	maturation	obfuscation	ossification
sequestration	trepidation	vituperation	volition

B. Complete. (1 point each)

1. All the spelling words take the form of _____.

2. The suffix –tion is more commonly used than _____.

C. Change each word below to an adjective. (1 point each)

1. circumlocution _____   2. inauguration _____

3. trepidation _____

D. Change each word below to a verb. (1 point each)

1. marginalisation _____   2. depreciation _____

3. gesticulation _____   4. obfuscation _____

5. abrogation _____   6. sequestration _____

7. asphyxiation _____   8. homogenisation _____

E. Rewrite the following words as plurals. (1 point each)

1. conflagration _____   2. vituperation _____

3. diminution _____   4. gesticulations _____

F. Divide the following words into syllables. (1 point each)

1. conflagration _____   2. depredation _____

3. ossification _____   4. inundation _____

5. equivocation _____   6. circumlocution _____

Score: /43   Pass: 34/43

© Valerie Marett
Coroneos Publications

Australian Homeschooling #568
Test Your Spelling 7 & 8

Section 2, Test 7: -tion

From your spelling list find the words that fit each definition below and then find the words in the word search. (1 point each definition)

```
N O I T A S I L A N I G R A M
O N O I T A R G A L F N O C A
I M A T U R A T I O N G L D B
T Q N O I T A C O V I U Q E R
A S P H Y X I A T I O N W P O
S E Q U E S T R A T I O N R G
I N O I T U N I M I D N T E A
N O I T U C O L M U C R I C T
E U N O I T A R U G U A N I I
G E S T I C U L A T I O N A O
O S S I F I C A T I O N P T N
M O A N O I T A R E P U T I V
O P P M T R E P I D A T I O N
H E T O B F U S C A T I O N E
N O I T A D N U N I C S E K Z
```

1. a process whereby the fat droplets from milk are emulsified and the cream does not separate _____

2. a large fire which destroys a great deal of land or property _____

3. a process of making hard or rigid, e.g., fossilise _____

4. the action of taking forcible possession of something _____

5. the repeal or abolition of a law, right or agreement_____

6. an overwhelming abundance of people or things, flooding _____

7. the action of making something obscure, unclear or unintelligible _____

8. a reduction in size, extent or importance _____

9. the process or state of being deprived of oxygen which can result in unconsciousness or death _____

10. a feeling of fear or anxiety about something that may happen _____

Score: /10   **Pass: 7/10**

© Valerie Marott
Coroneos Publications

Australian Homeschooling #568
Test Your Spelling 7 & 8

Section 2, Test 8: -y says short i, -city, -ly, -ally, -ph

A. Spell these words. (Adult to read. 1 point each.)

eccentricity	egocentricity	ferocity	paucity
perspicacity	specificity	veracity	
extensively	inquisitively	vehemently	vicariously
chronologically	misogynist	sympathetically	
apocryphal	cacophonous	choreography	diaphanous
paraphernalia	phlegmatic	philanthropic	sycophant
ephemeral	euphemism	euphoria	

B. Complete the following: (1 point per space)

1. The prefix eu- comes from the Greek and means _____, _____

    _____.

2. The suffixes –ous, -eous, -ose and –ise show the word is an _____

    meaning _____, _____.

C. Write the noun form of each adjective below: (1 point each)

1. apocryphal   _____   2. philanthropic _____

3. cacophonous _____   4. euphoria   _____

5. ephemeral   _____   6. phlegmatic   _____

D. Complete the following form. (1 point each)

	Noun	Adjective	Adverb
1.	specificity	_____	_____
2.	egocentricity	_____	_____
3.	perspicacity	_____	_____
4.	ferocity	_____	_____
5.	eccentricity	_____	_____
6.	_____	_____	chronologically

Score: /49   Pass: 40/49

Section 2, Test 9: -y says short i, -city, -ly, -ally, -ph

A. From your spelling list find the words that fit each definition. (1 point each)

1. a mild or indirect expression substituted for one considered to be too harsh or blunt when referring to something unpleasant or embarrassing   _____

2. loving one's fellow man, benevolent, humane   _____

3. in a forceful, passionate or intense manner, with great feeling   _____

4. conformity to facts, accuracy   _____

5. the quality of having a ready insight into things   _____

6. ill sounding   _____

7. the act of thinking only of oneself, without regard for the feelings or desires of others   _____

8. the presence of something in only small or insufficient quantities   _____

9. a story or statement of doubtful authenticity, although widely circulated as being true   _____

10. a person who dislikes, despises or is strongly prejudiced against women   _____

11. a deviation or curb of orbit from circularity   _____

12. the quality of being or relating uniquely to a particular subject   _____

13. in a way that follows the order in which events or records occurred   _____

14. in a way that is experienced in the imagination through the actions of another person   _____

B. Write an antonym for each word below. (1 point each)

1. eccentricity	_____	2. ferocity	_____
3. paucity	_____	4. ephemeral	_____

Score: /18   Pass: 14/18

Section 2, Test 10: -ial, -tial, -ate, eu-

A. Spell these words. (Adult to read. 1 point each.)

actuarial	colloquial	controversial	deferential
inconsequential	preferential	quintessential	tangential
attenuate	collaborate	corroborate	decimate
denigrate	disseminate	emulate	exacerbate
expurgate	importunate	inchoate	obdurate
promulgate	scintillate	substantiate	vacillate

B. Change the adjective to a noun. (1 point each.)

1. controversial _____
2. obdurate _____
3. inconsequential _____
4. tangential _____
5. preferential _____
6. actuarial _____
7. colloquial _____
8. importunate _____

C. Change the verb to a noun. (1 point each.)

1. vacillate _____
2. expurgate _____
3. collaborate _____
4. exacerbate _____
5. scintillate _____
6. decimate _____
7. attenuate _____
8. emulate _____

D. Write an antonym for each word below. (1 point each.)

1. inconsequential _____
2. colloquial _____
3. deferential _____
4. decimate _____
5. controversial _____
6. substantiate _____
7. importunate _____
8. obdurate _____

E. Write a synonym for each word below. (1 point each.)

1. exacerbate _____
2. scintillate _____

Score: /50   Pass: 38/50

Section 2, Test 11: -ial, -tial, -ate

A. Complete: (1 point each space)

1. The prefix con-, or com– means _____. Con-, com-, col– or coll–
   can also mean _____ or _____.

2. The prefix ex– means _____, _____, _____ or _____

B. From your spelling list find the words that fit each definition. (1 point each)

1. relating to the work of compiling and analysing statistics _____

2. provide evidence to support or prove the truth of _____

3. remove matter thought to be objectionable or unsuitable from a text or account _____

4. representing the most perfect or typical example of a quality or class _____

5. confirm or give support to a statement, theory or finding _____

6. just begun so not fully formed or developed, rudimentary _____

7. language that is not formal, used in an ordinary conversation _____

8. diverging from the previous course or line _____

9. make a problem or situation worse _____

10. criticise unfairly or denigrate _____

11. reduce the force, effect or value of _____

12. to give rise or be likely to give rise to public disagreement _____

13. spread widely _____

14. emit splashes of light or sparkle _____

Score: /21   **Pass: 17/21**

Section 2, Test 12: hy-, -sion, -eous, -cious

A. Spell these words. (Adult to read. 1 point each.)

hydrofoil	hyperbole	hyperthermia	hypoxia
condescension	digression	egression	interspersion
repercussion	suasion		
contemporaneous	erroneous	extraneous	heterogeneous
predaceous	spontaneous		
audacious	capricious	fallacious	loquacious
pertinacious	rapacious	tenacious	vivacious

B. Divide each word below into syllables. (! point each.)

1. audacious _____   2. extraneous _____

3. hypothermia _____   4. capricious _____

5. repercussion _____   6. predacious _____

7. contemporaneous _____

C. Complete each meaning below. (! point each space.)

1. The prefix per– means _____ or _____.

2. The prefix mal– means _____.

3. The prefix un– means _____, _____, or _____.

4. The prefix hyper– means _____.

D. Complete the following table. (1 point each space.)

	Noun	Adjective	Adverb
1.	_____	fallacious	_____
2.	_____	audacious	_____
3.	condescension	_____	_____
4.	_____	rapacious	_____
5.	_____	loquacious	_____

Score: /48   **Pass:** 36/48

© Valerie Marett
Coroneos Publications

Australian Homeschooling #568
Test Your Spelling 7 & 8

Section 2, Test 13: hy-, -sion, -eous, -cious

A. Find a spelling word to fit each definition below and complete the crossword.
(1 point each)

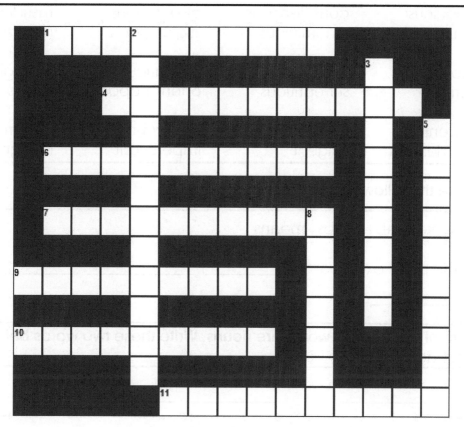

Across

1. unpredictable, subject to sudden changes in mood or behaviour
4. happening as a result of a sudden impulse
6. a temporary departure from the main subject
7. tending to talk a great deal
9. an exit or way out
10. a boat that is fitted with foils that lift the hull clear of the water at speed
11. irrelevant or unrelated to the subject being dealt with

Down

2. an unintended consequence of an action or event
3. showing an impudent lack of respect
5. based on a mistaken belief
8. persuasion as opposed to force or compulsion

B. Find a spelling word to fit each of the synonyms below. (1 point each)

1. superiority, haughtiness   _____

2. persistent, tenacious   _____

3. insatiable, gluttonous   _____

Score: /14   Pass: 11/14

© Valerie Marett
Coroneos Publications

Australian Homeschooling #508
Test Your Spelling 7 & 8

Section 2, Test 14: -ious, -oe says ee, -ent, -ment

A. Spell these words. (Adult to read. 1 point each.)

acrimonious	conscientious	disputatious	fastidious
gregarious	ignominious	litigious	multifarious
meritorious	nefarious	precarious	prodigious
salubrious	surreptitious	onomatopoeia	subpoena
abhorrent	belligerent	coherent	deterrent
embezzlement	exigent	impertinent	insurgent

B. Complete the following: (1 point each.)

1. The prefix ab– or abs– means _____, _____.

2. The prefix ex– means _____, _____, _____.
   _____.

C. Only two of the spelling words are nouns. Write these two words below.
   (1 point each.)

_____   _____

D. Write the verb form of each word below. (1 point each.)

1. abhorrent _____   2. litigious _____

3. deterrent _____   4. embezzlement _____

E. Change the grammatical form to fit what is requested below.
   (1 point each spce.)

Adjective	Noun	Adverb
1. acrimonious	_____	_____
2. fastidious	_____	_____
3. precarious		_____
4. exigent	_____	
5. belligerent	_____	_____
6. ignominious	_____	_____
7. meritorious	_____	_____

Score: /48   Pass: 38/48

© Valerie Marett
Coroneos Publications

Australian Homeschooling #568
Test Your Spelling 7 & 8

Section 2, Test 15: -ious, -oe says ee, -ent, -ment

A. From your spelling list find the words that fit each definition. (1 point each)

1. angry, bitter   manner _____

2. wishing to do one's work or duty thoroughly _____

3. deserving reward or praise _____

4. a writ ordering a person to attend court _____

5. pleasant, not run down, healthy _____

6. fond of having heated arguments _____

7. a theory or argument that is logical and consistent _____

8. a thing that discourages or intended to discourage someone from doing someone from doing something _____

9. not showing proper respect, rude _____

10. an action or activity that is wicked or criminal _____

11. the formation of a word from a sound associated with what is named, e.g., sizzle _____

12. having many varied parts or aspects _____

13. fond of company, sociable _____

14. remarkably or impressively great in extent or size _____

15. kept secret, especially as it might not be approved of _____

B. Write an antonym for each word below. (1 point each)

1. belligerent _____

2. gregarious _____

3. precarious _____

4. deterrent _____

5. fastidious _____

6. meritorious _____

7. coherent _____

8. surreptitious _____

9. conscientious _____

10. salubrious _____

Score: /25   Pass: 19/25

© Valerie Marett
Coroneos Publications

Australian Homeschooling #568
Test Your Spelling 7 & 8

Section 2 Test 16: -ent, -ence, -ance, -ous

A. Spell these words. (Adult to read. 1 point each.)

malevolent	negligent	reminiscent	truculent
acquiescence	complacence	credence	eloquence
precedence	reticence	turbulence	
aberrance	cognizance	exorbitance	malfeasance
obeisance	preponderance	protuberance	recalcitrance
ambiguous	assiduous	conspicuous	garrulous

B. Write an antonym for each spelling word below. (1 point each.)

1. ambiguous _____
2. malevolent _____
3. negligent _____
4. exorbitance _____
5. turbulence _____
6. complacence _____
7. eloquence _____
8. reticence _____

C. Find a spelling word that fits each list of synonyms below. (1 point each.)

1. consent to, permit, agree to _____
2. knowledge, realisation, recognition _____
3. talkative, verbose, chatty _____
4. similar to, comparable with _____
5. lump, swelling, bulge _____
6. careful, painstaking, conscientious _____
7. credibility, plausibility _____
8. noticeable, discernible _____

D. Change the following adjective to a noun. (1 point each.)

1. negligent _____
2. reminiscent _____
3. malevolent _____
4. truculent _____

Score: /43   Pass: 34/43

© Valerie Marett
Coroneos Publications

Australian Homeschooling #568
Test Your Spelling 7 & 8

A. From your spelling list find the words that fit each definition. (1 point each)

1. clearly visible, attracting notice or attention _____

2. departing from the accepted standard _____

3. an expression of deferential respect _____

4. the fact of being greater in number, quantity or importance _____

5. wrong doing, especially by a public official _____

6. eager or quick to argue or fight _____

7. having an obstinate, uncooperative attitude towards authority or discipline _____

8. belief or acceptance of something as true _____

9. having or showing a wish to do evil to others _____

10. showing great care and perseverance _____

11. open to more than one interpretation not clear or decided _____

12. knowledge or awareness of something _____

13. the avoidance of saying all one knows or feels or not saying more than is necessary _____

14. especially talkative, especially on trivial matters _____

15. the reluctant acceptance of something without protest _____

16. unreasonably high price or amount charged _____

17. priority in importance, order or rank _____

18. a feeling of smug or uncritical satisfaction with oneself or one's achievements _____

19. failure to take proper care of something _____

Score: /19   **Pass: 14/19**

Section 2, Test 18: -ous, -ise, -ize, -al, -ic

A. Spell these words. (Adult to read. 1 point each.)

abstentatious	congruous	gratuitous	meticulous
obstreperous	preposterous	presumptuous	scrupulous
scurrilous	ubiquitous	unctuous	vociferous
aggrandise	galvanise	ostracise	plagiarize
egotistical	empirical	inimical	paradoxical
aesthetic	altruistic	bureaucratic	cathartic
enigmatic	lethargic	mnemonic	vitriolic

B. Complete the following: (1 point each space.)

1. The prefixes in-, im-, il-, ir– mean _____. The prefixed in– and im– can

   also mean _____, _____, _____, _____.

2. The prefix magn– means _____.

3. The prefix sol– means _____.

C. Answer each question below: (1 point each.)

1. adverbial form of <u>magnanimous</u>   _____

2. noun form of the adjective <u>aesthetic</u>   _____

3. noun form of the verb <u>aggrandise</u>   _____

4. noun form of the verb <u>ostracise</u>   _____

5. adverbial form of <u>altruistic</u>   _____

6. noun form of the adjective <u>scurrilous</u>   _____

7. noun form of <u>vociferous</u>   _____

8. noun form of <u>lethargic</u>   _____

D. Divide each word into syllables: (1 point each.)

1. obstreperous _____   2. ubiquitous _____

3. paradoxical _____   4. mnemonic _____

Score: /47   Pass: 36/47

© Valerie Marett
Coroneos Publications

Australian Homeschooling #568
Test Your Spelling 7 & 8

Section 2, Test 19: -ous, -ise, -ize, -al, -ic

A. From your spelling list find the words that fit each definition. (1 point each)

1. form an idea about something _____

2. done suddenly without due care or consideration _____

3. increase the power, status or wealth of; enhance the reputation beyond what is justified _____

4. failing to observe the limits of what is permitted or appropriate _____

5. a system such as patterns, letters or ideas which assist in remembering something _____

6. take the work or idea of someone else and pass it off as one's own _____

7. unruly, hard to control _____

8. seemingly absurd or self-contradictory _____

9. present, or in several places simultaneously _____

10. expressing or characterised by vehement opinions _____

11. showing a disinterested and self-less concern for others _____

B. It is important not to confuse words. Write a sentence for each word below to show you understand their meaning. (2 point each)

1. ingenuous: _____

   _____

2. ingenious: _____

   _____

3. precipitous: _____

   _____

4. precipitate: _____

   _____

Score: /19   **Pass:** 14/19

Section 2, Test 20: -ible, -able, -ant, -ent

A. Spell these words. (Adult to read. 1 point each.)

contemptible reprehensible	feasible susceptible	incontrovertible	irascible
despicable	execrable	impeccable	inimitable
complaisant penchant	desiccant poignant	flagrant repugnant	nonchalant stagnant
benevolent munificent	despondent quotient	expedient petulant	indolent transcendent

B. Complete. (1 point each space.)

1. -ible and –able are commonly used to terminate _____ and
   generally add the idea of _____, _____,
   _____.

2. The prefix trans– means " _____, _____, _____. "

C. Write the three different ways insurgent may be used as a noun.
(1 point each.)

1. _____ 2. _____ 3. _____

D. Change each word below to a verb. (1 point each.)

1. despicable _____   2. desiccant _____

3. execrable _____

E. Change the following adjectives to nouns. (1 point each.)

1. poignant _____   2. insurgent _____

3. incontrovertible _____   4. expedient _____

5. contemptible _____   6. inimitable _____

7. complaisant _____   8. petulant _____

9. benevolent _____   10. irascible _____

11. munificent _____   12. repugnant _____

Score: /51   Pass: 40/51

© Valerie Marett
Coroneos Publications

Australian Homeschooling #568
Test Your Spelling 7 & 8

Section 2, Test 21: -ible, -able, -ant

A. **Find a spelling word to fit each definition below and complete the crossword.**
   (1 point each)

Across

4. extremely distasteful, unacceptable
5. deserving hatred and contempt
8. deserving censure or condemnation
9. showing a tendency to be easily angered
10. in low spirits from loss of hope

Down

1. hostile, aggressive
2. easily influenced by feelings or emotions
3. deserving contempt, despicable
6. extremely bad or unpleasant
7. a tendency to do something

B. **Write a synonym for each word below.** (1 point each)

1. indolent _____
2. stagnant _____
3. nonchalant _____
4. impeccable _____
5. transcendent _____
6. poignant _____

C. **Write an antonym for each word below.** (1 point each)

1. munificent _____
2. flagrant _____

Score: /18

Pass: 13/18

Section 2, Test 22: more y says ee, -ive, -ite, more –ic

A. Spell these words. (Adult to read. 1 point each.)

apathy	arbitary	consistency	extraordinary
frugality	implicitly	notoriety	parsimony
poignancy	subtlety		
derivative	interrogative	introspective	invective
pejorative	provocative	retrospective	vindictive
expedite	incite	plebiscite	
acoustic	bombastic	cataclysmic	catastrophic
choleric	ecliptic	egotistic	palaeontologic
pedantic	sceptic	spasmodic	thermodynamics

B. Complete: (1 point each space.)

1. The prefix re– means "_____, _____."

2. If "y" is the only _____ at the end of a word of more than one
   _____, the "y" says _____.

3. The prefix ec– means "_____, _____."

C. Two of the spelling words are verbs. Change them to nouns. (1 point each)

1. expedite _____   2. incite _____

D. Change the following nouns to adjectives. (1 point each)

1. pejorative _____   2. consistency _____

E. Write a synonym for each word below. (1 point each)

1. implicitly _____   2. invective _____

3. bombastic _____   4. sceptic _____

5. incite _____   6. pedantic _____

7. spasmodic _____   8. brevity _____

9. interrogative _____   10. provocative _____

11. parsimony _____   12. pejorative _____

Score: /60   Pass: 50/60

© Valerie Marett
Coroneos Publications

Australian Homeschooling #568
Test Your Spelling 7 & 8

Section 2, Test 23: more y says ee, -ive, -ite, more –ic

A. From your spelling list find the words that fit each definition. (1 point each)

1. relating to the branch of science concerned with fossil animal and plants _____

2. involving or causing sudden great damage or suffering _____

3. high sounding but with little meaning _____

4. irascible, angry _____

5. relating to a large scale violent event in the natural world _____

6. the branch of physical science that deals with the relations between heat and other forms of energy _____

7. lack of interest, enthusiasm or concern _____

8. relating to the sounds or sense of hearing in, for example, a building _____

9. originating from, based on or influenced by _____

10. a person inclined to question or doubt accepted opinions _____

11. looking back or dealing with past events or situations _____

12. the direct vote of all members of the electorate on an important public question, e.g., changing the constitution _____

13. make something happen quicker _____

B. Write an antonym for each word below. (1 point each)

1. vindictive _____   2. introspective _____

3. apathy _____   4. incite _____

5. derivative _____   6. incite _____

7. vindictive _____   8. bombastic _____

Score: /21   **Pass:** 17/21

© Valerie Marett
Coroneos Publications

Australian Homeschooling #568
Test Your Spelling 7 & 8

Section 2, Test 24: con-, -in

A. Spell these words. (Adult to read. 1 point each.)

concatenation	conceited	concede	concierge
conciliation	condone	confiscate	confiscate
conglomeration	connoisseur	conspiratorial	construe
contemplate	contemptuous	contravene	convoluted
inane	inconsequence	incoherent	incorrigible
induce	indulge	inertia	inference
innuendo	insipid	integral	intimation

B. Divide the following words into syllables. (1 point each)

1. conspiratorial _____
2. inertia _____
3. inconsequence _____
4. insipid _____
5. conglomeration _____
6. condone _____

C. Change the following verbs to nouns. (1 point each)

1. contemplate _____
2. indulge _____
3. confiscate _____
3. intimidate _____
5. contravene _____
6. condone _____

D. Change the following to the form indicated. (1 point each)

1. concatenation (v)_____
2. conspirator (v)_____
3. indulge (n)_____
4. contravene (n) _____
5. contemplate (n)_____

E. One of the spelling words is a plural noun. Write it below. Write the singular form. (1 point each space.)

_____   _____

F. Write sentences clearly showing the meaning of "intimate" and "intimidate." (1 point each sentence.)

_____

_____

Score: /53   **Pass: 43/53**

© Valerie Marett
Coroneos Publications

Australian Homeschooling #568
Test Your Spelling 7 & 8

Section 2, Test 25: con-, -in

A. From your spelling list find the words that fit each definition. (1 point each)

1. a number of different things, parts or items that are grouped together _____

2. of a person or their behaviour that is not able to be reformed _____

3. an allusive or oblique remark or hint that is typically suggestive or disparaging _____

4. relating to a secret plan made by a group of people to do something unlawful or harmful _____

5. an expert judge in matters of taste _____

6. a tendency to do nothing or to remain unchanged _____

7. to allow oneself to enjoy a particular pleasure _____

8. the act of mediation between two disputing people or groups _____

9. intricately folded, twisted or coiled, especially of a story or plot _____

10. showing scorn or derision _____

11. necessary to make a whole complete, essential _____

12. to take or seize with authority, e.g., customs _____

13. lacking vigour or interest _____

14. lacking sense or meaning, silly _____

15. offend, especially against a law or order _____

B. Write an antonym for each word below. (1 point each)

1. convoluted	_____	2. insipid	_____
3. intractable	_____	4. condone	_____
5. inane	_____	6. incoherent	_____
7. integral	_____	8. intrinsic	_____

Score: /23   **Pass: 18/23**

Section 2, Test 26: Mixed Spelling

A. Spell these words. (Adult to read. 1 point each.)

brusque	cajole	camaraderie	chameleon
demeanour	epicurean	exasperation	gourmand
iconoclast	juxtapose	maelstrom	misanthrope
nuance	opprobrium	paradigm	placebo
plethora	sanguine	sequester	silhouette
succinct	surfeit	verbatim	vicissitude

B. Divide the following words into syllables. (1 point each)

1. nuance _____
2. misanthrope _____
3. epicurean _____
4. opprobrium _____
5. maelstrom _____
6. camaraderie _____
7. vicissitude _____
8. brusque _____

C. Write a synonym for each word below. (1 point each)

1. demeanour _____
2. opprobrium _____
3. maelstrom _____
4. gourmand _____
5. misanthrope _____
6. sequester _____

D. Write an antonym for each word below. (1 point each)

1. succinct _____
2. verbatim _____
3. surfeit _____
4. cajole _____
5. plethora _____
6. brusque _____
7. opprobrium _____
8. sanguine _____

E. Three of the spelling words can be used as both a noun or a verb. Write them below. (1 point each)

1. _____
2. _____
3. _____

F. Eight of the spelling words can be used as a noun. Write three of them below. (1 point each)

1. _____
2. _____
3. _____

Score: /52   Pass: **44/52**

© Valerie Marett
Coroneos Publications

Australian Homeschooling #568
Test Your Spelling 7 & 8

Section 2, Test 27: Mixed Spelling

A. Find a spelling word to fit each definition below. Find the word hidden in the hidden word puzzle. (1 point each definition)

E	S	E	Q	U	E	S	T	E	R	M	E	Q	S	T
P	Q	M	T	G	H	V	U	Z	N	I	S	S	A	N
I	N	U	J	T	A	M	H	J	R	T	O	D	N	I
C	O	E	I	E	E	K	W	E	N	A	P	S	G	C
U	E	M	P	V	M	U	D	W	U	B	A	P	U	C
R	L	D	U	O	O	A	O	T	T	R	T	M	I	U
E	E	E	X	I	R	C	N	H	X	E	X	O	N	S
A	M	M	U	A	R	H	A	U	L	V	U	R	E	U
N	A	E	M	C	H	B	T	T	A	I	J	T	U	R
E	H	A	F	I	A	E	O	N	I	N	S	S	Q	F
J	C	N	B	S	G	Q	L	R	A	O	C	L	S	E
A	R	O	H	T	E	L	P	O	P	S	N	E	U	I
E	D	U	T	I	C	C	I	V	J	P	I	A	R	T
P	A	R	A	D	I	G	M	M	K	A	O	M	B	R
D	N	A	M	R	U	O	G	O	B	E	C	A	L	P

1. mutual trust and respect among people who spend a lot of time together _____

2. harsh criticism or censure _____

3. a connoisseur of good food; a person who enjoys eating and often eats too much _____

4. a damaging loss of valuable people or resources _____

5. a person who dislikes humans and avoids their society _____

6. in exactly the same words that were used originally _____

7. a typical example or pattern of something _____

8. persuade someone to do something by coaxing or flattery _____

9. a large or excessive amount of something _____

10. briefly and clearly expressed, (written or spoken) _____

11. the use of ambiguous language to obscure the truth _____

12. a person devoted to sensual enjoyment, especially food and drink _____

Other words hidden in the puzzle are: brusque, demeanour, chameleon, surfeit, juxtapose, maelstrom, placebo, sanguine, sequester, silhouette.

Score: /12   **Pass:** 8/12

Section 2, Test 28: Important Foreign Terms

These foreign words are in common usage. Write the meaning of the word or phrase below. Write on a separate paper if necessary(1 point each phrase.)

1. à la carte: _____

2. ad hoc: _____

3. bona fide:_____

4. carte blanche: _____

5. caveat emptor: _____

6. erratum: _____

7. habeas corpus: _____

8. ibid: _____

9. in absentia: _____

10. in extremis: _____

11. in lieu: _____

12. per annum: _____

13. per capita: _____

14. persona non grata: _____

15. prima facie: _____

16. pro rata: _____

17. quid pro quo: _____

18. quod erat demonstrandum (QED): _____

19. status quo: _____

20. sub judice: _____

21. tete a tete: _____

22. vis a vis :_____

Score: /22   Pass: 16/22

Answers Test Your Spelling 7 & 8

Page 3: Test 1
1. qu   w   wh
2. consonant   long i   long e
3. vowel
4. el
5. drop the f   v
6. j
7. s
8. a, o, or u;   i or e;   short vowel
9. short vowel
10. c   the long ee sound
11. short vowel
12. drop the e   beginning with a
    vowel, e.g., hope   hoping
13. —able   —ous
14. es
15. es   s
16. y

Page 4: Test 2
B. Review Rules
1. vowel.
2. prefix   base word
3. base word   suffix   vowel
4. between   first two
C. Divide into syllables
1. as/sas/in/ate
2. ap/pal
3. an/tic/i/pa/tion
4. ac/quit/tal
5. al/leg/a/tion
6. cal/lous
D. Complete the table
1. fascination (noun) fascinating (adj.)
2. alleged (adj)   allege (v)
3. appreciation (n) appreciative (adj)
4. admirer (n)   admire (v)

Page 5: Test 3
A. Definition
1. callous
2. appal
3. atrocious
4. analysis
5. anticipation
6. assent
7. caricature
8. acquisition
9. adjudicate
10. acquittal
B. Rules
Any order
1. to, toward, near, in addition to, by
2. long e sound
3. state, office, function   cause to be,

a kind of state
4. without

Page 6: Test 4
B. Base words
1. critic
2. benefit
3. connect
4. conscious
5. buoy
6. bewilder
C. Definition
1. conceived
2. buoyancy
3. consequences
4. bilateral
5. boycott
6. consciousness
7. bureaucracy
8. brevity
9. benevolent
10. bequeath
11. commotion

Page 7: Test 5
A. Rules
1. with, together, jointly
2. not, against
3. life
B. Turn into adjectives
1. bureaucratic
2. conscious
3. buoyant
4. beneficial
5. consequential
C. Turn into adverbs
1. consequently
2. convincingly
3. believably
4. conceivably
D. Add prefix un—
Any order
1. unconvincingly
2. unbelievably
E. Synonyms
1. believable
2. critical
3. convince
4. brevity
5. curiosity
6. bludgeon
F. Antonym
1. complimentary
2. indifference

© Valerie Marett
Coroneos Publications

Australian Homeschooling #568
Test Your Spelling 7 & 8

Answers Test Your Spelling 7 & 8

Page 8: Test 6
B. Complete
1. syllable   ee sound
2. with, thoroughly, fully
3. a vowel

C. Antonym
1. resistance
2. conciliate
3. deficit
4. deviate
5. diminish
6. conceit
7. deleterious
8. censure
9. deceptive

D. Suffix –tion
1. deviation
2. conciliation
3. conceptualisation
4. deception
5. interception
6. vaccination
7. dilapidation

E. Syllables
1. de/let/er/ious
2. dis/guis/ed

Page 9: Test 7
A.   Synonym

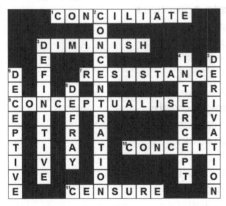

B. Add "ed" and "ing"
1. censured   censuring
2. resisted   resisting
3. defrayed   defraying
4. concentrated   concentrating

Page 10: Test 8
B. Complete:
1. out of   from   thoroughly   former
   c, p, q, s, t.
2. one who, that   condition
3. in make into   to put into   to get into
   enmesh

4. resembling   relating to

C. Antonyms
1. durable
2. emigrate
3. exhausted
4. disagreeable
5. extravagance
6. eccentricity
7. excruciating
8. exaggeration
9. disastrous
10. elementary

D. Adjectives
1. embarrassing
2. exaggerated
3. eccentric
4. extravagant

E. Sentence
Parent to check.

Page 11: Test 9
A. Synonyms
1. duress
2. extraordinary
3. distinguished
4. excruciating
5. eloquent
6. eccentricity
7. distributed
8. embezzle
9. durable
10. disastrous

B. Other meanings
1. embezzlement: a criminal offence in which an employee steals from his employer
2. duress: a criminal defence which asserts the defendant was forced to commit the offence against his or her wishes because of a threat of force.
3. estuary: the part of the mouth or lower course of a river in which its current meets the sea tides and is subject to their effects.

C. Syllables
1. ex/cru/ci/a/ting
2. dur/ess
3. dis/a/gree/able
4. el/o/quent
5. dynamics
6. extravagance

Page 12: Test 10
B. Complete
1. out of, from, thoroughly or former
   c, p ,q ,s, t
2. before at the front
3. away   off

Answers Test Your Spelling 7 & 8

C. Legal, geographical or English meanings
1. **geology:** the science that deals with the structure of the Earth, especially of the rocks of which it is formed.
2. **encyclopaedia:** a book, or series of books giving information on general or specific branches of knowledge, which is usually arranged alphabetically
3. **fiord:** a narrow arm of the sea, with steep cliffs on either side
4. **fraud:** the offence of obtaining a material benefit by false representations or pretences

D. Only adjectives
Any order
1. excruciating
2. exquisite
Parent to check sentences

Page 13: Test 11
A. Synonym
1. eccentricity
2. farcical
3. forfeit
4. garble
5. gaiety
6. exuberant
7. germane
8. exquisite

B. Antonym
1. uniformity
2. irrelevant
3. listless
4. gentle
5. honest
6. invigorate

C. Definition
1. fascinating
2. exorbitant
3. forecast
4. ferocious

D. Plurals
1. eccentricities
2. estuaries
3. encyclopaedias

Page 14: Test 12
B. Complete
1. not   without   b, m and p
2. in   into   towards   inside
3. the prefix   the base word   the base word   suffix   vowel
4. over   beyond   above   exceedingly   to excess
5. under   beneath
6. blood

C. Difference between words
1. **harangue:** noisy, strong-worded speech, often full of blame for the listener.
2. **harass:** to trouble by repeated attacks, to disturb continually.

D. Syllables
1. hid/e/ous
2. im/med/iate/ly
3. guar/an/tee
4. haem/or/rhage

Page 15: Test 13
A. Definition
1. heinous
2. indulge
3. hypocrisy
4. hierarchy
5. haemorrhage
6. gauge
7. immediately
8. instantaneous
9. glossary

B. Antonym
1. stupidity
2. ugly
3. beautiful
4. sincerity
5. real
6. strict

C. Homonym
horde   hoard
horde: a great company, a multiude
hoard; to gather together, e.g., food or money, for future use

D. Change to adverbs
1. instantly
2. intelligently

Page 16: Test 14
B. Complete
1. beginning   end of a word
2. wrong   bad   erroneous   lack of   not
3. great   huge 10_6 of a given unit

C. Other meanings
1. **monologue:** a poem, dramatic piece etc. in which a single person speaks alone; a form of dramatic entertainment by a single speaker.
2. **legislation:** law created by Parliament; also known as statute law.
3. **meridian:** an imaginary line on the earth's surface passing through the Poles and any given point on the earth's surface and cutting the equator at right

Answers Test Your Spelling 7 & 8

angles.

4. **jurisdiction**: the power of the Court to hear matters.
5. **megabyte:** a measure of data or memory equivalent to approximately one million bytes which is a unit of storage.
6. **misdemeanour**: a minor offence
7. **judgement**: the decision of a judge in a case and the reason for the decision

Page 17: Test 15
A. Synonyms
1. juvenile
2. necessity
3. liquefy
4. nautical
5. luscious
6. manoeuvre
7. liable
8. magnificent
9. meticulous
10. miscellaneous

B. Change to an adjective
1. jurisdictional
2. manoeuvrable
3. necessary
4. meridinal
5. jealous
6. natural

C. Change to adverb
1. meticulously
2. necessarily
3. magnificently

D. Homonym
1. **liable:** open or subject to something possible or likely, especially something undesirable, e.g., liable to be hurt.
2. **libel:** damage to a person's name or reputation by written or printed matter; the crime of printing such matter.

E. Correct Sentence
Parent to check.

Page 18: Test 16
B. Complete
1. with   together
2. for   forward
3. at the end of a syllable
4. not

C. Complete passage
1. monotonous   oppressive
2. proficiency
3. nocturnal   nuisance   coercion
4. idiosyncratic   innocuous

5. cognisant
6. notoriety   potential
7. spontaneous   solicitude   onerous

Page 19: Test 17
A. Antonym
1. inept
2. congruous
3. sense
4. unpronounceable
5. insecure
6. diurnal
7. varied or interesting

B. Synonym
1. solicitude
2. obliterate
3. spontaneity
4. potential
5. incongruous
6. coercion
7. nuisance
8. onerous

C. Adverb
1. spontaneously
2. nocturnally
3. solicitously
4. oppressively
5. notoriously
6. complacently
7. proficiently
8. monotonously

D. Syllables
1. cog/nis/ant
2. ob/lit/er/ate
3. o/ner/ous
4. sol/i/ci/tude

Page 20: Test 18
B. Complete
1. without u
2. four
3. do again   back or backwards
4. having the quality of relating to
5. look or see
6. under below from secretly instead of

C. Synonym
1. separable
2. realise
3. passable
4. rough, twisted
5. scrupulous
6. regularly
7. recurrence
8. quiescent

Answers Test Your Spelling 7 & 8

9. simultaneous
10. responsible

D. Similar meanings
scrupulous   particular

Page 21: Test 19
A. Antonyms
1. passable
2. scrupulous
3. regularly
4. separable
5. recurrence
6. quiescent

B. Definition
1. application
2. quadruplicate
3. sarcasm
4. farcical
5. recommendation
6. quorum
7. articulate
8. quiescent
9. scrupulous
10. simultaneous

C. Adverbs
Any order
1. regularly
2. reluctantly

D. Base word
1. recommend
2. apply
3. special
4. scruple
5. farce
6. recur

Page 22: Test 20
B. Complete
1. not, against, opposite
2. not enough   not done well   below
not done as much as is necessary
3. time
4. hold
5. across   beyond   change
6. to twist
7. under   below   from   secretly
instead of

C. Geographical Meaning
Any order.
1. **topography**: a detailed description and
analysis of the geographical features of a
small area.
2. **tributaries:** streams flowing into a larger
stream or river.
3. **trough**: a relatively low area of pressure.

or a low depression or hollow between
waves.

Page 23: Test 21
A. Definitions
1. uncorroborated
2. superstitious
3. unanimous
4. subsequent
5. temporarily
6. umbrage
7. treachery
8. tyranny
9. synonymous
10. tranquillity

B. Sentences showing meaning
Answers will vary. Suggestions below.
1. The boy lay <u>unconscious</u> on the road and
we were unable to revive him.
2. John embezzled all of his wards inher-
itance and we considered his behaviour
<u>unconscionable</u>.

C. Antonym
1. pronounceable
2. permanently
3. gradually
4. conscious

D. Adjectival form
1. sudden
2. temperamental

Page 24: Test 22
B. Definition
having the quality of, relating to
C. Plurals
1. hypotheses
2. curricula
3. criteria
4. radii
5. strata
6. formulae
7. antitheses
8. termini or terminuses

D. Sentences
Answer will vary. Parent to check.
Suggestions.
1. The money was distributed to the states
on a per capita basis so they all received
different amounts.
Admission as a group is $10 per head.
2. The school principal headed the morn-
ing assembly.
The principle is important. I am not pre-
pared to compromise.
3. Many newspapers show a bias towards

Answers Test Your Spelling 7 & 8

3. Many newspapers show a bias towards female politicians.
Australians, in general, are not prejudiced against other nationalities.

Page 25: Test 23
A. Definition
1. versatility
2. radius
3. equitable
4. vicinity
5. criterion
6. perpetually
7. hypothesis
8. impel
9. voracious
10. antithesis

B. Synonyms
1. curriculum
2. compel
3. variegated
4. vague
5. terminus
6. vengeance
7. effective

Page 26: Test 24
B. Complete
1. —ible   —ibly
2. —able   —ably
3. whole words   whole words minus their final e   whole words whose final y is changed to one

C. Correct adjective
1. justifiable
2. suppressible
3. integrity
4. distraction
5. corrupt
6. expand
7. inflame
8. distraction

Page 27: Test 25
A. Complete word
1. eligible
2. capable
3. irritable
4. memorable
5. amiable
6. legible

B. Definition
1. deprecate
2. inflammable
3. prospective

4. ingenuous
5. combustible
6. luxuriant
7. commendation
8. detract
9. toleration
10. exhaustion

C. Antonym
1. denial
2. cheerful
3. union
4. intolerable
5. honesty
6. prohibition

D. Synonym
precipitate

Page 29: Test 1
Common Rules
1. vowel
2. power
3. down, with
4. add "s"   change "y" to "i" and add "es"   "s"
5. fully, with   together
6. into, on, near   towards
7. not, opposite of, reverse, separate, deprive of,   away
8. over, in excess
9. under, below,   slightly
10. before   for, forward
11. not, against, opposite
12. back, again
13. great   one
14. across, beyond, change
15. people, populace, population

Page 30: Test 2
B. Syllables
1. com/ple/ment/ary
2. des/ul/tory
3. du/plic/ity
4. tau/tol/ogy
5. oph/thal/mol/ogy
6. quand/ary

C. Noun, verb, adjective or adverb?
nouns

D. Explain the difference
1. **complementary**: that which completes something
2. **complimentary**: something given or supplied without charge; **or** a polite, or flattering comment

E. Complete the chart.
1. austere (adj)   austerely(adv)

© Valerie Marett
Coroneos Publications

Australian Homeschooling #568
Test Your Spelling 7 & 8

2. conciliatoriness (n) conciliatorily (adv)
3. desultoriness (n) desultorily (adv)
4. congruous (adj)
5. disparate (adj) disparately (adv)
6. morphological (adj)
   morphologically (adv)
7. gullible (adj)   gullibly (adv)

Page 31: Test 3
A. Word Meanings
1. tautology
2. rudimentary
3. disparity
4. proclivity
5. duplicity
6. morphology
7. quandry
8. desultory
9. probity
10. alacrity
11. congruity
12. gullibility

B. Plurals
1. ideologies
2. complementaries
3. quandaries
4. congruities
5. perversities
6. tautologies

C. Antonym
Answers may vary slightly
1. uncomplimentary
2. prosperity
3. complimentary
4. cynicism, suspicion

Page 32: Test 4
B. Complete
1. Y   long i sound
2. more than one   long e
3. suffix   y
4. consonant   y to i   and add es.

C. Plural
1. ignominies
2. synecdoches
3. eponyms
4. idiosyncracies
5. acronyms
6. corollaries

D. Antonyms
1. cause, origin
2. honour
3. optimism
4. self-government
5. hellish
6. lethargic

Page 33: Test 5
A. Definition
1. oxymoron
2. dichotomy
3. cryptic
4. paroxysm
5. synecdoche
6. androgynous
7. eponym
8. cynicism
9. hegemony
10. acronym
11. trichotomy
12. calumny

B. Synonym
Answers may vary slightly
1. folk law, tradition
2. energetic, vigorous
3. division, separation, gulf, chasm
4. individualistic, distinctive
5. blissful, ideal
6. recurrent, repeated

Page 34: Test 6
B. Complete
1. nouns
2. -sion

C. Adjectives
1. circumlocutory
2. inaugural
3. trepidatious (or trepidacious)

D. Verb
1. marginalise
2. depreciate
3. gesticulate
4. obfuscate
5. abrogate
6. sequester or sequestrate
7. asphyxiate
8. homogenise

E. Plurals
1. conflagrations
2. vituperations
3. diminutions
4. gesticulations

F. Syllables
1. con/fla/gra/tion
2. dep/re/da/tion
3. os/sif/i/ca/tion
4. in/un/da/tion
5. e/quiv/o/ca/tion
6. cir/cum/lo/cu/tion

Answers Test Your Spelling 7 & 8

Page 35: Test 7
Definitions
1. homogenisation
2. conflagration
3. ossification
4. sequestration
5. abrogation
6. inundation
7. obfuscation
8. diminution
9. asphyxiation
10. trepidation

N	O	I	T	A	S	I	L	A	N	I	G	R	A	M
O	N	O	I	T	A	R	G	A	L	F	N	O	C	A
M	A	T	U	R	A	T	I	O	N	G	L	D		B
T	Q	N	O	I	T	A	C	O	V	I	U	Q	E	R
A	S	P	H	Y	X	I	A	T	I	O	N	W	P	O
S	E	Q	U	E	S	T	R	A	T	I	O	N	R	G
N	N	O	I	T	U	N	I	M	I	D	N	T	E	A
M	O	I	T	U	C	O	L	M	U	C	R	I	C	T
E	U	N	O	I	T	A	R	U	G	U	A	N	I	I
G	E	S	T	I	C	U	L	A	T	I	O	N	A	D
O	S	S	I	F	I	C	A	T	I	O	N	P	T	N
M	O	A	N	O	I	T	A	R	E	P	U	T	I	V
O	P	P	M	T	R	E	P	I	D	A	T	I	O	N
H	E	T	O	B	F	U	S	C	A	T	I	O	N	E
N	O	I	T	A	D	N	U	N	I	C	S	E	K	Z

Page 36: Test 8
B. Complete
1. good, well, happily
2. adjective — having the quality of relating to

C. Noun
1. apocrypha
2. philanthropy
3. cacophony
4. euphoric
5. ephemera or ephemeron
6. phlegm

D. Adjective, Adverb
1. specific (adj)   specifically (adv)
2. egocentric (adj)   egocentrically (adv)
3. perspicacious (adj)   perspicaciously (adv)
4. ferocious (adj)   ferociously (adv)
5. eccentric (adj)   eccentrically (adv)
6. chronology (n)   chronological (adj)

Page 37: Test 9
A. Definition
1. euphemism
2. philanthropic

3. vehemently
4. veracity
5. perspicacity
6. cacophonous
7. egocentricity
8. paucity
9. apocryphal
10. misogynist
11. eccentricity
12. specificity
13. chronologically
14. vicariously

B. Antonym
1. conventionality
2. gentleness
3. abundance
4. permanent

Page 38: Test 10
B. Adjective to noun
1. controversialist
2. obduracy
3. inconsequentiality
4. tangentiality
5. preferentiality
6. actuary
7. colloquialism
8. importunity

C. Verb to noun
1. vacillation
2. expurgation
3. collaborator or collaboration
4. exacerbation
5. scintillation
6. decimation
7. attenuation
8. emulation

D. Antonym
Answers may vary slightly
1. consequential
2. standard, formal
3. disrespectful
4. create
5. uncontroversial
6. disprove
7. undemanding
8. gentle, yielding

E. Synonym
Answers may vary slightly
1. aggravate, intensify
2. shine, sprakle

Page 39: Test 11
A. Complete
1. fully   with   together

© Valerie Marett
Coroneos Publications

Australian Homeschooling #568
Test Your Spelling 7 & 8

Answers Test Your Spelling 7 & 8

2. out of   away from   lacking   former
B. Definition
1. actuarial
2. substantiate
3. expurgate
4. quintessential
5. corroborate
6. inchoate
7. colloquial
8. tangential
9. exacerbate
10. denigrate
11. attenuate
12. controversial
13. disseminate
14. scintillate

Page 40: Test 12
B. Syllables
1. au/da/cious
2. ex/tran/eous
3. hypo/therm/ia
4. ca/pri/cious
5. re/per/cus/sion
6. pred/a/cious
7. con/temp/or/an/eous
C. Complete.
1. through, intensive
2. bad (or badly)
3. not, against, opposite
4. over
D. Complete the table
1. fallacy (n)
   fallaciously (adv)
2. audaciousness (n)
   audaciously (adv)
3. condescending (adj)
   condescendingly (adv)
4. rapaciousness (n)
   rapaciously (adv)
5. loquacity or loquaciousness (n)
   loquaciously

Page 41: Test 13
A. Crossword (see top next column)
B. Synonym
1. condescension
2. pertinacious
3. voracious

Page 42: Test 14
B. Complete
1. away from   off
2. out of   away from   lacking   former

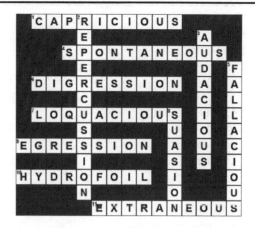

C. Nouns
Any order.
1. onomatopoeia
2. subpoena
D. Verbs
1. abhor
2. litigate
3. deter
4. embezzle
E. Change the grammatical form
1. acrimony (n)   acrimoniously (adv)
2. fastidiousness (n) fastidiously (adv)
3. precariously (adv)
4. exigence or exigency (n)
5. belligerence (n) belligerently (adv)
6. ignominy (n)   ignominiously (adv)
7. merit (n)   meritoriously (adv)

Page 43: Test 15
A. Definition
1. acrimonious
2. conscientious
3. meritorious
4. subpoena
5. salubrious
6. disputatious
7. coherent
8. deterrent
9. impertinent
10. nefarious
11. onomatopoeia
12. multifarious
13. gregarious
14. prodigious
15. surreptitious
B. Antonym
Answers may vary slightly
1. peaceful
2. unsociable, reserved
3. safe, secure
4. incentive
5. careless, disorganised

6. discreditable
7. incoherent
8. open, honest
9. casual, lazy
10. unpleasant

Page 44: Test 16
B. Antonym
Answers may vary.
1. unambiguous
2. benevolent
3. careful
4. reasonable, cheap
5. peace, calmness
6. dissatisfied
7. inarticulacy
8. friendliness
C. Synonym
1. acquiescence
2. cognizance
3. garrulous
4. reminiscent
5. protuberance
6. assiduous
7. credence
8. conspicuous
D. Adjectives to nouns
1. negligence
2. reminiscence
3. malevolence
4. truculence

Page 45: Test 17
A. Definition
1. conspicuous
2. aberrance
3. obeisance
4. preponderance
5. malfeasance
6. truculent
7. recalcitrance
8. credence
9. maelovent
10. assiduous
11. ambiguous
12. cognizance
13. reticence
14. garrulous
15. acquiescence
16. exorbitance
17. precedence
18. complacence
19. negligent

Page 46: Test 18

B. Complete
1. not   into on near towards
2. great
3. alone
C. Write the answer
1. magnanimously
2. aestheticism
3. aggrandisement
4. ostracism
5. altruistically
6. scurrility
7. vociferousness
8. lethargy
D. Syllables
1. ob/strep/er/ous
2. ub/iqu/i/tous
3. par/a/dox/i/cal
4. mnem/on/ic

Page 47: Test 19
A. Definition
1. conceptualise
2. precipitous
3. aggrandize
4. presumptuous
5. mnemonic
6. plagiarize
7. obstreperous
8. paradoxical
9. ubiquitous
10. vociferous
11. altruistic
B. Sentences
Parents to mark.
To help, definitions are shown below.
1. **ingenuous**: innocent and unsuspecting actions
2. **ingenious**: clever, original , inventive
3. **precipitous**: dangerously high or steep
4. **precipitate**: cause to happen suddenly, unexpectedly

Page 48: Test 20
B. Complete
1. adjectives   capable of
   allowed   worthy of
2. across   beyond   change
C. insurgent as a noun
Any order.
1. insurgent
2. insurgence
3. insurgency
D. Change to verbs
1. despise

2. desiccate
3. execrate

E. Change to nouns
1. poignancy
2. insurgence or insurgency
3. incontrovertibility
4. expedience or expediency
5. contempt
6. inimitableness
7. complaisance
8. petulance
9. benevolent
10. irascibility
11. munificent
12. repugnancy

Page 49: Test 21
A. Solve the crossword

B. Synonyms
Answers may vary slightly.
1. lazy, slothful
2. motionless, still
3. calm, relaxed
4. flawless, faultless
5. superior, predominant
6. touching, sad

C. Antonym
Answers may vary slightly.
1. mean
2. unobtrusive

Page 50: Test 22
B. Complete.
1. back   again
2. vowel   syllable   ee
3. out of   outside of

C. Change verb to noun.
1. expediter or expedition

2. incitement

D. Change noun to adjective.
1. pejoratively
2. consistent

E. Synonyms
Answers may vary.
1. eccentricity
2. abuse, vituperation
3. briefness, pithiness
4. cynic
5. inflame, provoke
6. precise
7. sporadic, infrequent
8. briefness
9. searching, inquisitorial
10. infuriating
11. meanness, miserliness
12. derogatory, disparaging

Page 51: Test 23
A. Definitions
1. palaeontologic
2. catastrophic
3. bombastic
4. choleric
5. cataclysmic
6. thermodynamics
7. apathy
8. acoustic
9. derivative
10. sceptic
11. retrospective
12. plebiscite
13. expedite

B. Antonyms.
Answers may vary.
1. forgiving
2. extrovert
3. enthusiasm
4. dissuade
5. original
6. suppress
7. forgiving
8. straight-forward

Page 52: Test 24
B. Divide into syllables.
1. con/temp/or/an/eous
2. in/er/tia
3. in/con/se/quence
4. in/sip/id
5. con/glom/er/at/ion
6. con/done

C. Change verbs to nouns
1. contemplation
2. indulgence

3. confiscation
4. intimidation
5. contravener or contravention
6. condonation

D. Change nouns to verbs.
1. concatenate
2. conspire
3. Indulgence
4. contravention
5. condescend

E. Plural and singular noun
indices   index

Page 53: Test 25
A. Definition.
1. conglomeration
2. incorrigible
3. innuendo
4. conspiratorial
5. connoisseur
6. inertia
7. indulge
8. ciliation
9. convoluted
10. contemptuous
11. integral
12. confiscate
13. insipid
14. inane
15. contravene

B. Antonym
Answers may vary.
1. straightforward
2. interesting
3. compliant
4. condemn
5. sensible
6. coherent
7. incidental, peripheral
8. extrinsic

Page 54: Test 26
B. Divide into syllables
1. nu/ance
2. mis/an/thrope
3. epi/cu/rean
4. op/prob/ri/um
5. mael/strom
6. cam/ar/ad/erie
7. vic/is/sit/ude
8. brus/que

C. Synonym
Answers may vary
1. bearing, manner
2. vilification, abuse

3. whirlpool
4. glutton
5. hermit
6. isolate

D. Antonyms
Answers may vary
1. verbose
2. imprecise
3. lack, dearth
4. bully
5. scarcity
6. verbose, polite
7. praise
8. pessimistic

E. Both noun and verb
Any order.
1. nuance
2. silhouette
3. surfeit

F. Nouns
Any of the following
camaraderie, chameleon, epicurean,
gourmand, maelstrom, misanthrope,
silhouette, iconoclast

Page 55: Test 27
Definitions

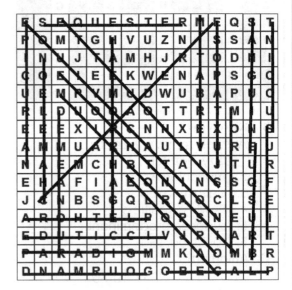

1. camaraderie
2. opprobrium
3. gourmand
4. haemorrhage
5. misanthrope
6. verbatim
7. paradigm
8. cajole
9. plethora
10. succinct

11. equivocation
12. epicurean

Page 56: Test 28
Important foreign terms
1. from the menu: referring to food being ordered as separate items
2. created or done for a particular purpose as necessary
3. genuine, real
4. complete freedom to act as one wishes
5. principle that the buyer alone is responsible for checking reliability and suitability of goods before purchase
6. an error in printing or writing
7. a writ requiring a person under arrest to come before a judge or court, especially to secure their release if there are unlawful reasons for detaining them.
8. in the same source, i.e., book named previously
9. while not present at the event being referred to
10. at the point of death
11. instead of
12. for each year
13. for each person
14. an unacceptable or unwelcome person
15. based on the first impression; accepted as so unless proven otherwise
16. proportionally
17. a favour or advantage granted in return for something
18. it is proved (used to convey that a fact or situation demonstrates the truth of one's theory or claim, e.g., in maths)
19. the existing state of affairs, especially relating to political matters
20. under judicial consideration and therefore prohibited from being discussed
21. a private conversation between two people
22. in relation to; in regard to